FOREX TRADING GUIDE

TABLE OF CONTENT

16.	Forex prediction and trading method

17.	Forex megadroid robots and meta trader.

INTRODUCTION

The people who have a flair for investment seek all the necessary information that can directly or indirectly affect their investment decisions. There are a lot of points that has to be taken in to consideration before investing in to the foriegh exchange markets. Because a simple mistake or underestimated factor can cause you severe damages. Some of the guiding steps that can direct you towards the success include the forex reviews. A forex review is just like an important part of information that is very well important to be known in advance and one can get maximum benefits out of using it. These reviews are available in to the form of updates hat you can get in order to know the actual position of different currencies.

Nowadays there is a significant increment observed in the number of people investing in to foreign exchange market. But rarely a few of them secure high profits and reason behind their success is their planning and analytical skills. The people who are new to the forex market or even the older ones also need the forex reviews that can help them better. A forex review can not only tell you the hottest currency of the day but with the help of the frequent forex reviews you can also get the fluctuations that are taking place in a particular currency. A forex review is thus important to be considered as it can give you better understanding of the actual market condition.

With the recent advancements in the information technology and in the telecommunication sector, getting these forex reviews has become really simple. The internet has resulted in to a reliable source of getting the forex reviews. Apart from this, there are various news channels that give you the current updates and the forex review at your place just by sitting in front of your television sets. Another way of getting the forex review is to subscribe the alerts or updates of the foreign exchange market. So in a way it can be said the television sets, cell phones, newspapers and internet are some of

the important sources of getting such
reviews.

CHAPTER ONE

A trader is someone who places orders on the financial market. This could be on behalf of financial institutions, such as big banks, investment funds and hedge funds, or as an independent trader.

Exchange orders, such as buying or selling stocks, are either in the trader's own name, or on behalf of clients or for the financial institution or broker that employs them. There can be further categorisation, depending on the assets being traded: Forex, equities, bonds, commodities, etc.

Traders who work for financial institutions or brokers buy and sell shares on behalf of their employer's clients, not with their own money. This means that rather than making a profit or a loss on their actual trading, they earn a salary as a trader. In this case, the trader takes virtually no risk in the market - it is on their customer buying or selling financial instruments to cover the risk. The trader's clients may be anything from individuals to companies that do not have a trading room of their own.

Those who trade on their own personal account are using their own money to attempt to earn profit for themselves. These accounts are funded with their personal funds and trades are executed through online trading platforms. Even though online brokers offer leverage, the amounts traded by home traders are much smaller than those of a professional trader. Since online trading is often done on the OTC (Over the Counter) market, the success of traders in their own accounts are only estimates.

Defining Success as a Profitable Forex Trader

Now that you know what a trader is, how can you become a trader? And then, how do you become successful at it?

When starting to trade, it is important to understand what you want to achieve from it, and how you define success.

What are some points to keep at the forefront when learning how to become a Forex trader?

Set yourself a realistic and quantifiable goal. This could be something along the lines of, achieving a 20% annual return on your investment, or reaching a total of 100 pips per month.

Your goal should also be easy to measure.

Set a goal that can be achieved over a long time frame - it is recommended to set an annual goal to achieve rather than a monthly goal.

Once you have set your main trading goal for the year, it is now time to start learning how to achieve it.

Identify what resources are available to you.

How much money are you able to use as a starting deposit?

Do you want to become a full time Forex trader? Or are you just looking to trade on the weekends?

These are some of the questions you should be asking yourself.

Once you have a clear vision, it is time to make your action plan. This plan should include the currency pairs you are planning to trade and the number of daily trades you are going to commit to.

CHAPTER TWO

Learn Currency Trading

Most people find that the field of forex trading is very interesting. It is due to the fact that every day you will across different situations that one has to deal with. Thus if have so much interest then the currency forex learn online trading is the best way from where you can acquaint yourself with the latest information and what is going in the market. The learn currency trading includes the knowledge of the currencies and how the exchange takes place. Thus all the currencies related aspects come under the learn currency trading. With the currency forex learn online trading you can practically see how the trading is carried out and what the things that you should keep in mind are.

The currency forex learn online trading also helps you in providing the information about the stock exchange as well. It will deal with the aspects like rates that prevail in the market and the how the changes are occurring and what are the things that are been affected by this change. So the currency forex learn online trading will guide with all the different issues. Even the learn currency trading wilt how light on the currencies and the way they are to be dealt with. Apart from the learn currency trading you can also learn about the stocks as well which is very important. Therefore you will find a complete package of information through where you can update yourself.

The learn currency trading will help to understand the conversion of the different currencies and at the same time you will also come to know the differences and the conditions that go while the exchange are done. Similarly the currency forex learn online trading is also the same thing where you can have all the minute details that you want to know about the forex market or the foreign exchange. The forex market is the mobile market where things are changing within seconds and you cannot predict what will happen in the next few seconds. Hope the information given you to regarding the trading is up to the mark so that the users can benefit from it.

The Forex market or foreign exchange market is known to be the world's largest and most powerful currency trading platform which involves dozens of countries. Hundreds of financial centers from around the world act as anchors to trade among the numerous buyers and sellers. Operating around the clock with the exception of weekends, Forex Trading is done by people of all trades. The primary purpose of the Forex market is to assist international investment and trade by means of currency conversion. Supporting price speculation and "carry over" is an added benefit of the foreign exchange market.

Forex trading is a great way to earn Money through investments in various currencies. Traders from across the world constantly purchase and sell currencies in order to gain a profit from their transaction. They implement various strategies to make sound investments in this market. Apart from self predictions, they also take advice from forex brokers and other intelligent investors to spot an opportunity. Forex for beginner investors can be quite confusing. You need to watch and practice first, before making any investment. There are various forex trading games available on the internet that do not require any money to play. Once you get the basic idea of forex trading, try your hand at these games before actually investing in the real market.

To give you example, suppose you run the metrics on your system and find that your winning percentage is currently 48%. You've got an idea on how to improve it to 53%, which you "think" would increase your overall returns. Next would be to run the analysis on the system with the change on real market data. By looking at the results, you can see if this change accomplished it objective, but also if there were trade-offs in other aspects of your system performance, such as a lower profit-to-loss ratio. You then can make a calculated decision on whether you should incorporate the change or not.

Summary. Trading is a process from which you wish to have consistent – and reliable – results. Spotting, entering and executing trades is an activity that you repeat on a regular basis, so consistent profits is your desire, focus on making your actions consistent.

Forex for beginners can either prove to be profitable or they can bear heavy loses depending on their strategy, frame of mind or volatility in market conditions. It is always advisable to invest small sums of money when you are just starting out in forex trading. This can limit your chances of bearing huge losses in case you make a wrong trade.

CHAPTER THREE

Even in the forex market you have the fore brokers who help the people to give them reliable information. Therefore the forex broker reviews are taken from various people so that one can get an idea which one is suitable and who is the most experienced person. The forex broker review includes the knowledge and the experience they hold. The forex broker comparison is done to get the ideal forex broker reviews about the brokers of the forex market. So if the forex broker comparison it is liable that will work hard to provide better services to their clients. So it is important that the forex broker review is taken in order to choose the best broker you want for your transaction. To know all about the forex broker reviews and the forex broker comparison you can read this article.

The forex broker reviews are also done to analyze the performance whether the quality is maintained or not. So for the forex broker review the forex broker comparison is also done in order to get the most efficient and proficient broker in the market. Though a fee is charged from the clients but still the people go to the friends and other people to find out the forex broker review about the various brokers who are the part of the forex market. So if you want that your transaction is carried out by safe hands then it is equally necessary that some arrangements are made for it.

Therefore it can be summed up that the forex broker review is very necessary for the people who are new to this business. Also the forex broker reviews are not only important for the new businessman but also for the othr people in case they want to seek advice from them. Thus the forex broker comparison can be the best way through which you will be able to find a capable broker for your business so that you do not make a wrong decision. Therefore one must understand the need of a broker in such a business where everything is changing within seconds. So must be fully aware of all the conditions.

The best forex broker is one who is experience and has sufficient knowledge to deal even with the critical problems of the currencies. The work of a best forex brokers is that they help their customers in guiding them about the right decision. They also guide them about the rates and the schemes that can be availed. Therefore the broker forex trading together with the best forex brokers can be a great combination for the clients as they will be able to get efficient services. The best forex broker must have certain qualities that may them special and always in demand. So it can be said that the broker forex trading is a bit difficult but if it is understood properly then no one can beat you.

The broker forex trading includes the investments and the stock market as well. So you can say that the broker forex trading is one of the best way to carry out the transactions. Therefore the best forex broker will help you in the best possible way. So with the help of the best forex brokers you can get the required information about the forex market. Thus it is better to have the best forex broker so that they can guide and help you to create a platform for the new people and also allow their clients to make profits. Therefore it is important that you hire the best forex brokers in order to earn the profits for yourselves.

Investing in the best scheme is quall important as it is to find the best forex brokers. It is not at all an easy task to find a best forex broker as you may be misguided also by some of the people. So it is necessary that you find a reliable person who has enough knowledge to sort out your problems. With the help of the broker forex trading the clients are able to establish cordial relationships with the other people also who can help them whenever they need their help. Thus all what is important is that the broker should be qualified and apart from that they should be proficient as they are the backbone of the clients.

CHAPTER FOUR

Auto Forex Trading

The auto forex trading includes the system which is automated so that the profits in the business are increased. The automated forex system trading is just like a simple program which is designed in such a way that it can tell you about the changing trends of the market. So with the help of the automated forex system trading you can know whether the prices are increasing or decreasing over a period of time. Therefore the auto forex trading is more of software that aims in providing the current status of the market whether it is related to the rats or some other relevant information. In this article you will come to know how thus automated system works and with what efficiency.

The auto forex trading is done so as to improve the quality as well as the quantity of the information. With the use of the internet increasing to such a great extent it is important that the forex market is converted in to the automated forex system trading so that you can fetch better results. The updating in anything is done just to enhance the performance. Therefore the automated forex system trading is the best way to get a good performance ratio in the business and it will also help you in gaining more profits in the business. The auto forex trading provides them the best means through which the entire system can be controlled using a simple software program.

The auto forex trading will help the clients as well as the customers to get the required information which they want to get. Even the slightest change in the market will be depicted by using the automated forex system trading. Therefore the overall conclusion is that in the age when internet has become so fast it is important that the system is updated just for the betterment of the lives of the people. Only if such changes are made only then you can progress in life. As it is always said that someone has to start a new trend then why not to believe in ourselves and start the amazing and new trend which is beneficial.

If you're not fully armed with this information it can be very scary and intimidating, because what many new traders do not understand is that a huge percentage of those that are new lose money in the marketplace, and they lose it quickly.

Only a small percentage make any money. What you should be able to discern when reading between the lines that means the small percentage is making all of that income from all of the trades that the others are losing! This is literally millions of dollars!

Forex trading is profitable... very profitable... and now you can earn from the online exchanges too.

CHAPTER FIVE

Forex Platforms

The forex platform is nothing but a platform that works for the welfare of the clients. The main purpose of the forex platforms is that it helps in providing mobility to the clients. Therefore by using the forex trading platform you can provide efficient services to the customers so that they are satisfied. With the forex trading platforms becoming so popular the use of the forex platforms is increasing day by day. Though the services offered by different forex platform is different but still people the most perfect forex platform which can understand their needs and help them to invest in the best scheme. Thus through the forex trading platforms you can give excellent services to the clients with the forex platforms.

The forex trading platform is the means or a place which is made by the brokers through which the customers can contact the broker and also take suggestions from them through the forex platforms. But the advantage of using the forex platform is that the people are able to get some god options. With the forex trading platforms you will understand the customers well and in a more coordinated way. Therefore those brokers who wish to avail good services use the forex trading platform as the forex trading platforms are very useful in establishing connection with the clients. Therefore according to the type of service that you want you can chose the best and most suited forex trading platform for yourselves.

The forex trading platform is usually of four types which differ in the services and the mobility which is given to the customers. So depending upon the benefits the users choose the forex trading platforms. If you like the services are comfortable with the money also then you can definitely avail he services through the forex platforms. The forex platform is surely a platform where you can learn a lot of things and at the same it will teach you to deal with the different type of people and the competition going in the market. Thus one can think of about all the benefits and then choose the best platform that suites them and appeals them the most.

CHAPTER SIX

Automatic Forex Trading and software
The automated forex trading system is one of the main components of the forex trading. The automatic forex trading has become so common because lots of users are finding it good and so the demand of the forex automated trading is increasing day by day. So has become important that the forex automated trading becomes more used platform by the people. With the automated forex trading system the people can avail the online facility where they can get all the information by just sitting at home. Due to this reason the automatic forex trading has gained popularity and so the people

want that such systems are developed which are useful to the people.

The automatic forex trading is not a website but a software program that is developed using the latest technology in order to furnish the information to the customers. In the automated forex trading system regularly updates are done so that the users only have the latest information which will help them always ahead of the other people. In order to be a member on the automated forex trading system you just have to create your user id and password will be generated through which our can access your own account. So with the help of the forex automated trading one can get the entire information by just spending few minutes on the internet. Thus the forex automated trading or the automatic forex trading have the same purpose as they are one and the same thing.

The automatic forex trading can be really beneficial to the traders who have sufficient knowledge about this. As it will bring fruitful results therefore it is important that the forex automated trading is carried ou on large scale. Initially it can be on a smaller scale but later the automated forex trading system can be easily expanded with the help of the other members and slowly and slowly it will fare well. Thus the entire system has to be finely built so that there are no problems later. So all the people who are interested in the software applicability then they can surely engage in such task.

The automated forex trading software is the software that is used to collect the relevant information about the rates and the market conditions. With the forex auto trading software the users are able to log in to their personal account and then in out the condition of the shares and the currencies. The currency trading software is used to check the market value of a particular currency. Therefore whether it is the currency trading software or the forex trader pro all come under the category of the forex market and so have to be dealt with security. Through the automated forex trading software the mobility increases and then it is easy to manage the customers. Thus the forex auto trading software is an efficient tool which is used in the forex market.

The forex auto trading software is very useful as you can access the information using the internet. With the automated forex trading software one will be able to acquire all the information within few seconds. Therefore one can see that there are several benefits or the advantages of using the automated forex trading software together with the currency trading software also. Even the forex trader pro has many benefits with respect to the forex auto trading software. Thus it is obvious that the technology has greatly improved the conditions of the market with forex trader pro taking its place. Therefore must not forget the advantages that you will come across while using this software.

The forex trader pro has the main work which consists of the assistance to the traders. The forex trader pro is one of the highly used programs. Thus there is no doubt that the forex auto trading software is the recognized program used for the welfare of the users. You can also use the currency trading software if you want to particularly deal with the currencies. It is one of the specialized programs that are prepared by the forex department. Thus it can be concluded that the automated forex trading software and the currency trading software are highly developed tools which will provide you to overcome the problems that are being faced by the people during the manual processing.

CHAPTER SEVEN

Forex Mini Account

The forex mini account is an account that is opened with a minimum account balance. The forex trading accounts are marked by special features that include the small amount and at the same time they have o face either huge gain or huge loses. Therefore the forex trading accounts can be beneficial only if invested in the right company. If you do not have enough knowledge about these types of accounts then you can also use the forex demo account through which you can learn how the transaction is carried out. The forex demo account option is available online and so there is no difficulty in finding it.

But the forex mini account can be opened with about $10 to $25 is the least amount through which the account is started.

The forex mini account is a special type of account that can be opened by anyone but the amount should be less. Thus the forex trading accounts are the best way if you want to start some sort of business activity. So with the help of the forex demo account you can learn the tactics which are needed when such types of accounts are opened. Therefore if you are looking for some good option then nothing could be better than the forex trading accounts. The forex demo account will guide to from the initial stages to the final stages. Therefore the forex mini account can be easily set up with the help of the broker and the reputed organization.

The forex mini account will not only earn you good profits but at the same tie if proper attention is not paid thn you are bound to suffer huge loses also. Therefore it is advised to use the forex demo account first so that you do not commit any mistake when the transaction is carried out. This is the best way as there will be no problems then. So are you still confused with the forex trading accounts then you can try this option as it will help you and also the broker to a large extent if good profits are made by the company or the organization.

CHAPTER EIGHT

Forex Courses and charts

In order to have the complete knowledge of the forex market forex courses are arranged so that the interested people can learn something new through these forex trading courses. The forex course or the forex trading course is a course that deals with the minute details of the forex market. During the forex course you will be taught the basic things that one may need. Therefore the whole idea of introducing the forex courses or the forex trading courses is to make more people aware about the various aspects of the forex market. So to know more about the forex trading course you can read this article which gives you brief information about the different forex courses.

The forex courses include the courses like the management skills, technical skills and the interpersonal skills which are very important in this field. Apart from the skills the forex course also deals with the knowledge which is the key in the entire market. One needs to grasp each and every thing during the forex trading course so that they are able to satisfy the customers. Even the forex trading courses provide you with a path though which you can make your career. Thus the whole concept is that the forex trading courses are beneficial for the new students and alos for those who want to increase their knowledge about the forex course or the forex trading course.

Another important issue regarding the forex courses or the forex trading course is that it is a field where you need to be practical and at the same time aware of what is going in to the market. It is the need to be attentive so that a proper solution is available to the clients. Therefore with the help of the experience faculty the forex course will fetch you with the best results. So what are you waiting for then if you also want to become a successful broker in the forex market then you can also undergo the forex trading courses to enhance the skills so that all the customers are satisfied with you which brings more clients to the company for which you are working.

The forex chart is a chart that depicts the market conditions. Most probably the forex chart denotes the rise and the fall in the prices. The forex charts are used so that the customers and the company holders can get a idea as to what is the current rate of the currencies going. It is important to be updated about the forex charts because with the help of these charts one will be able to calculate the gain or loss that they have incurred during the whole transaction. These charts are the best way to know about all the changes that are going in the market. So if you do not know about these charts and the purpose of using then just read this article where you will find all the information.

The forex charts is an exciting thing that has been devise by the forex market. With the help of the forex charts you know the current status and then by studying the current position you can invest in any of the deals you want. Therefore it is equally important to study the forex chart which can guide with all the changes that have occurred and due to which reasons. So one can understand how necessary it is to know about the forex chart and the way to look at it. Thus if one is able to understand the forex market then it is sure that they will never commit the mistake and always be in profits.

The forex chart is the main aspect apart from the rates and the automated trading software. With the use of the forex charts you an easily determine what is going in the market and what will be the result of the next few days. It is all because that you have enough experience that you are able to predict the future prospects of the forex market. It is all due to the understanding of the forex market. Thus if you also want that you should be able to understand the market then it is necessary that you be attentive and at the same time responsible enough to shoulder the responsibility.

CHAPTER NINE

Forex Market Trading Hours and pairs
The forex market trading is one of the most important fields where you will come to know about the various trading ways and how to become an efficient trader. The forex market trading includes the forex market hours and the forex markets. The forex trading hours means the amount of time taken to change the rates. The forex trading times are same throughout the country as the same rules are followed everywhere. Therefore the forex trading times remain constant. The forex market hours are of a specified duration which includes the forex trading hours. Even the forex markets have to be

studied well during the forex market hours. Therefore for more information about the forex markets and the forex market trading read this article.

The forex market trading is done to get the overview about what is happening in the market. But this entire work has to be completed within the forex market hours which consist of the forex trading times and the forex trading hours. The forex markets survey has to be done to check whether everything is working right or not. These surveys are useful in predicting the current status and the causes of the changes that occur every day. The forex markets also throw light on the different marketing strategies which are used by the brokers to attract the customers. Therefore you can deal with all the different things.

With the forex trading hours and the forex trading times you can get enough time to deal with all the matters.

Therefore the forex trading times are very advance due to the changes that have occurred. Despite the forex trading hours you can also use the forex market hours for carrying out any of the task that you want. It is necessary to do this as it is needed to know the people and their requirements. So with the forex markets evolving at a faster pace you can definitely get profits by this work. Therefore the forex market trading has to be studied well if you want to survive or else you will have to face tough competition which is very difficult to bear.

Three ways to hone your skills as a part-time trader include:

1. Find the Right Pairs to Trade

Although forex trading occurs 24 hours a day throughout the week, it's best to trade during peak volume hours to guarantee liquidity. Liquidity is a trader's ability to sell a position, which is much easier when the market is most active. Assuming that you work a nine-to-five job, you'll be available for trading either early or late in the day. Depending on the currency pairs you're trading, high volume may occur at either end of those timeframes to conduct trades.

For small traders with mini accounts and beginners who lack experience, trading U.S. currency against various foreign currencies is advised. The great majority of dollar volume traded on forex markets occurs in the currency pairs below. It may be wise for part-time traders to restrict trading to these briskly-traded currencies due to the strong liquidity in these pairs.

USD/EUR
USD/JPY
USD/GBP
USD/CHF
USD/CAD
USD/AUD

For part-time traders with more experience and time to research conditions and circumstances that may impact currency prices, the following pairs also offer high liquidity:

EUR/GPB

EUR/JPY

EUR/CHF

Experts advise trading only the USD/EUR pair for the part-time trader who has a limited trading window. This pair is most frequently traded and there's an abundance of readily available information on these currencies across all forms of media.

Conversely, experts discourage part-timers from trading two foreign pairs that may require more sophisticated knowledge and lack the same level of information as the USD/EUR pair.

2. Set Up an Automated Trading System
Part-time traders may opt to trade on their own or choose an automated trading program to make trades for them.

There's a variety of automated trading programs with a full spectrum of functions available on the market. Some of them may be able to monitor currency prices in real-time, place market orders (impose limit, market-if-touched, or stop orders), recognize profitable spreads, and automatically order the trade. Please note, however, that even if a trade is ordered, there's no guarantee that the order will be filled on the trading floor at the price expected, especially in a fast-moving, volatile market.

A so-called "set and forget" program may be the best way for a beginning part-time forex trader, which allows the software to make automated decisions. Several automated programs offer a simple "plug and play" capability—an easy way for part-time beginners to start trading. This is one of the major benefits of automated trading—it offers disciplined, unemotional trades. Experienced part-timers may prefer a more hands-on trading approach by selecting automated trading software with more programmable options.

3. Apply Disciplined Decision-Making

Discipline and dispassion are essential for success for traders who spurn automated systems to make their own decisions. Part-time traders are advised to take profits when they materialize instead of anticipating wider spreads and bigger profits. This requires a degree of self-discipline in fast trending markets where favorable spreads can widen. Successful traders take profits when they can because a trend can turn around instantly due to unforeseen external events such as the financial crisis in 2008, and more recently, the onset of the COVID-19 pandemic. Trailing stop and stop market orders may be imposed to protect against sudden market reversals and to minimize risk, but as mentioned previously, there's no guarantee that an order will be filled at the anticipated price.

Part-time traders with little or no experience are advised to start trading small amounts of currency. By opening a mini forex account, which requires a smaller-than-standard cash deposit, traders can control 10,000 currency units (the standard currency lot controls 100,000 units of currency). Minimum cash deposits for a mini account may start at $10 and can be as high as $10,000.

CHAPTER

TEN

Forex Strategies and tips

The forex strategies or the forex trading strategies are the strategies which are used to improve the existing conditions of the market. In order to provide the best services you need to be efficient in dealing with people. Therefore each and every company has certain forex strategy which they us to attract the clients. The forex trading strategy is the principles that are laid down by the company and are used b the traders and brokers to appeal the customers so that they subscribe for the services of that particular company. The forex trading strategy also helps in making the services better. The quality is improved if the forex strategies or the forex trading strategies are used. Therefore all the brokers who want to get more customers must rely on the best forex strategy. For more details about the forex strategy read this article which is must.

The forex strategy is another name given for the objectives or the parameters which are laid down so that they can be entrusted and used whenever needed. For better features one must have forex strategies as they are the backbone of the strong reputation of the company. Almost all the companies have their own forex trading strategies which are followed and also the forex trading strategy is changed from time to time. It all depends upon the market and the conditions which are there in the market. Therefore the forex strategies or the forex trading strategy all have their own features which can be utilized for the betterment of the clients.

The forex trading strategy can serve the purpose that you are looking for. The forex strategy is just like the guidelines which are used by the company in order to help the customers achieve their aim of investing in any company. So if you use the forex strategies you will be able to understand what the customers need from the organization and will be able to get more customers with best forex trading strategies. Thus all the people who wish that they have lots of profits then they have to go for the most ideal forex trading strategies which are not only beneficial but also prove useful in the long run.

Successful Forex traders think differently from the rest. They aren't concerned with needing a high win rate or trying to trade every day regardless of market conditions.

In this post, I'm going to share with you nine of the top qualities that the best Forex traders in the world possess. What follows is a combination of lessons I've learned since I began trading in 2002.

So without further ado, let's begin!

What Does It Mean to Be Successful?
So Who Are the World's Best Forex Trader?

1. They Don't 'Lose'

2. They Use Price Action

3. They Have a Defined Trading Edge

4. Successful Forex Traders Don't Try Too Hard

5. They Think in Terms of Risk

6. They Don't Need the Money

7. Successful Forex Traders Know When to Walk Away

8. They Don't Focus on Wins and Losses

9. They Never Gave Up

What Does It Mean to Be Successful?

Before we get into the nine attributes, I want to clarify how we will define success in this article.

Any story about a successful Forex trader must include consistent profits. I think we can all agree that most traders use profits to benchmark the success of another.

However, success in any endeavor is about more than just money. It's also about the joy and passion it adds to your life.

This is one thing I can't teach. I can offer help in drawing key levels, determining trend strength and price action signals. However, I cannot teach passion.

You either love trading or you don't. There is no in between. So the question is if you don't have a passion for trading, can you really be successful?

Think about that for a moment. If you don't absolutely love what you're doing every day, can any amount of money make you content?

I would argue that it can't.

So as you're reading today's post, remember that it isn't just about the money. If your only reason for trading is making money, then you may want to have another look at your chosen career.

It's your passion for trading, not money, that will push you through the tough times. Without passion and a love for trading, no amount of money can make you a successful Forex trader.

So Who Are the World's Best Forex Traders?
Stanley Druckenmiller
Portrait of Stanley Druckenmiller
Stanley Druckenmiller has long considered George Soros his mentor.

He indicated that the "very large sums" of money were making it difficult to make big profits for investors.

Bill Lipschutz

I've written about Bill Lipschutz in the past.

He's known for turning $12,000 of inheritance money into $250,000 while still in college.

He did this by investing the risk capital in his free time.

However, nobody is perfect, and Bill is no exception.

Shortly after turning $12,000 into $250,000, he made one bad investment decision that nearly cost him the entire account. He was back to square one.

Time is a risk factor. A three to one reward to risk ratio is acceptable for trades of 48 hours or less, but longer duration trades require a five to one ratio.

The game is the "thing". According to Bill, a truly successful trader has got to be involved and into the trading; the money is the side issue.

Know pain, but don't fear it. You have to feel the pain of a bad trade, or a wrong trade. If you don't and are numb to it, then it's over.

Insane focus is a must! Bill Lipschutz once said "when they call you crazy, you know you are on the right track. He was referring to the work ethic and insane focus required to succeed as a Forex trader.

Now that we've covered some of the world's best Forex traders, let's discuss the nine attributes they share.

1. They Don't 'Lose'

Man making trading losses

Before the emails start pouring in, let me explain...

No Forex trader is without losses. But there's a distinct difference between how the beginning trader loses and how the best Forex traders lose.

What's the difference?

Mindset.

Most starting out in the Forex market view a loss as a bad thing. It's a way of signaling that they did something wrong.

And doing something wrong is bad. At least that's what we've come to believe over the course of our lives.

However, the successful trader doesn't view a loss as a "bad" thing.

It's also not something the market did to you. The Forex market doesn't know where you entered or where your stop-loss order is located.

Unlike you, the market is always neutral. So when you lose, it's a matter of reflecting on what you could have done better.

Don't get me wrong, nobody likes to see a trade go against them. I don't care if you've been trading for one month or ten years, it's always more enjoyable to make money than to lose it.

That being said, just because a trade doesn't go your way doesn't mean you should take it personally. Thinking this way will only dig you a deeper hole.

The successful Forex trader has the mindset that a loss is simply feedback.

It's the market's way of disproving a trade setup. That's the only thing the Forex market has the ability to do because it doesn't know anything about you or where you entered the market, nor does it care.

Losses can be a powerful way to learn. Just remember that even a trade that ends up as a loss can be the right decision.

How is that possible, you ask?

If you've defined your edge, and the setup met all of your criteria to enter the market, then you did all you can do. The rest is up to the market, and some days the market just doesn't play along.

Next time you have a loss, take it as constructive feedback. Analyze the situation to see how you can improve the next time. Keep in mind, though, that even an A+ setup doesn't always work out.

I've had many trade setups that didn't work out that I would gladly take every single week.

That's because I know that my edge will win over time and put money in my account. In fact, a good exercise after a losing trade is to ask yourself, "would I take this same setup again next week if it presented itself?"

You should always be able to answer this question with a resounding "yes".

If you answer with a "no", you need to take a step back, determine where things went wrong and correct it for the next trade.

Start seeing trading losses as business investments rather than upsetting events. Each loss is an investment in your trading business and ultimately your trading education.

The money you put at risk on any given trade, whether it's $5 or $500, is an investment with the best Forex coach in the world—the market. Keep an open mind and it'll show you everything you need to know.

2. They Use Price Action
Price action trading with candlestick chart
Every successful Forex trader I've met uses price action in some way, shape or form.

This doesn't mean they're using price action in the same way I use it, but they are using some form of price action as part of their trading strategy.

Whether a trader is using raw price action or simply using it to identify key levels in the market, price action plays a major role in any strategy.

That's because it serves as a representation of the psychology within a market. It gives us some insight into the minds of other traders.

Having some idea of where buy and sell orders are located in the market is critical to becoming the best Forex trader you can be. It can strengthen any trading strategy by providing areas to watch for potential entries as well as profit targets.

Trading Forex without using some form of price action is like trying to drive a car with one eye closed. It can be done, but I wouldn't recommend it.

So even if you are developing a strategy based on indicators, it would behoove you to learn about price action. If nothing else, it will provide a solid foundation from which you can design and develop other strategies.

3. They Have a Defined Trading Edge
Man getting a competitive advantage
I see a lot of talk on the internet about the need for a trader to develop an edge and define it. And, if I'm honest, most of what I've read out there is pretty alarming.

It's little wonder why so many traders struggle to understand what an edge is and how they can develop one of their own.

So what exactly is a trading edge and why is it important?

An edge is everything about the way you trade that can help put the odds in your favor.

It's a combination of the time frame you trade, the price action strategies you use, the key levels you've identified, your risk to reward ratio, and other factors. It even includes your pre- and post-trading routine.

How do you handle losses? What do you do when you win? These are all things that make up your trading edge.

Think about it like this...

What allowed Brazil to win so many World Cups in soccer (football to most of the world)?

Was it the passing? Maybe the shooting?

It was everything. Brazil had the "total package", as they say. It was their passing, shooting, dribbling, movement of the ball, set plays and everything in between that gave them an edge over other teams.

Your trading is no different.

Although there are dozens of factors that make up your edge, you don't have to master all of them at once. Nor do you have to master all of them to start putting the odds in your favor.

It's better to master one set of factors and then slowly expand to others to further define your edge. Not only is this a natural progression, it's the preferred way to learn.

Have you heard the saying, "jack of all trades, master of none"?

If you try to master too many of these factors at once, you're setting yourself up to become good (not great) at a lot of things. That isn't what we want.

Instead, master one thing at a time. For example, become an expert at identifying key levels. Then expand your skill set by learning how to determine trend strength. After that, set your focus on learning about pin bars.

Those three things are all you need to witness a rise in your profit curve. Continue to expand your skill set in this manner and soon you will have a trading edge of your own.

The key is to only tackle one or two factors (at most) at a time. Using a slow and steady approach will get you on the road to becoming a successful Forex trader in no time.

4. Successful Forex Traders Don't Try Too Hard

Woman taking a break from work
But trying hard is what it takes, right?

Not quite.

This might apply to other ventures in life, but Forex is the exception. Successful Forex traders know that trying too hard is a sign that something isn't right.

This is different from studying hard. As a new trader to Forex, studying the market is highly recommended.

For instance, you can't spend too much time learning the ins and outs of the various currency pairs, or how to draw key levels. The harder you try to learn those particular topics, the better.

However, trying to make a trading strategy work will only lead to destructive behavior, such as emotional trading. Similarly, trying too hard to find trading opportunities is a good way to lose money on subpar setups.

When I first started trading Forex, I remember spending countless hours studying setups over the weekend. I would often come back to my trading desk multiple times on Saturdays and Sundays.

Then on Monday, more often than not I would end up taking a completely different trade setup only to watch the original trade idea move in the intended direction without me.

Does that sound familiar?

It happened because I was trying too hard. As soon as I stopped over-analyzing trade setups and trying to make them work, my profit curve started to rise.

Now I spend maybe 20 to 30 minutes per day looking at my charts—the exception being the charts I post on this website, of course.

As counterintuitive as it may seem, learning to not try so hard was one of the things that completely changed my trading career for the better.

Successful Forex traders have taken note of this, which is why they let the market do the heavy lifting for them.

5. They Think in Terms of Risk

Trading risk

It's often the smallest things in life that generate the greatest improvements.

The concept of thinking in terms of money risked, as it applies to Forex trading, is no exception. It's an extremely simple concept that can have a huge impact on your journey to becoming a top Forex trader.

I've never met a successful Forex trader who doesn't calculate their risk before putting on a position.

You may think that's an obvious statement, but a surprising number of traders don't think about how much money is at risk before opening a trade.

This is because they're using an arbitrary percentage to calculate risk, such as one or two percent of their trading account balance.

Think about your last trade for a moment. Did you define the exact dollar amount at risk before putting on the trade? Or were you more focused on the number of pips and the percentage of your account at risk?

The convenience of Forex position size calculators has made it so that we never have to consider the dollar amount being risked. This convenience has caused a huge oversight.

Don't get me wrong, I use the position size calculator at the link above before each and every trade.

However, I'm just as interested in the dollar amount at risk as the percentage of my account balance.

Aren't those the same?

Yes and no.

Obviously, 2% of $5,000 is $100. In that respect, the 2% and the $100 are essentially the same things.

However, in terms of the way our mind perceives these two figures, they're at opposite ends of the spectrum.

When you calculate your risk as a percentage only, you're defining your risk but you aren't accepting it.

As soon as you convert that percentage to a dollar amount, your mind is able to visualize what $100 looks like. This enables you to determine if you're prepared to lose that $100. In other words, is the trade setup in question good enough for your $100?

It's much easier to risk 2% without fully accepting the potential loss because it doesn't carry the emotional value that money does.

The best Forex traders know this. That's why they always define their risk in terms of a percentage and a dollar amount.

6. They Don't Need the Money
Money falling around man

There aren't many guarantees in the Forex market. But one guarantee I can make is that there's no successful Forex trader who is trading today for money he needs tomorrow.

In other words, trading Forex to gain a certain amount of money within a specific time period.

I'm not saying that you can't generate the majority of your income from trading Forex and do it full time. Such a statement would contradict my own experience.

What I am saying is that no successful Forex trader needs a win today to pay the electric bill tomorrow.

No trader can sustain that kind of pressure and become consistently profitable. That type of environment will only foster destructive emotions such as fear and greed.

This topic takes us back to the notion that the best Forex traders don't try too hard.

If you need the money from trading to pay bills, odds are that you'll feel pressured to win. If you're feeling pressured to win you'll most certainly be trying too hard instead of allowing the market to do the heavy lifting.

The bottom line is this...

You should only trade with money you're prepared to lose. Don't trade with the money you need to pay rent or provide for you or your family.

Similarly, don't allow the money to be your sole reason for trading. The desire for money is probably what attracted you to trading in the first place, but don't let it be your only desire.

Embrace the challenge and focus on the journey to becoming a successful Forex trader and the money will follow.

Let money be the byproduct of good trading.

7. Successful Forex Traders Know When to Walk Away
Walking away from work
Of course, I'm referring to taking a brief hiatus, not walking away for good.

All successful Forex traders know when to walk away and take a break. Those who are truly passionate about trading Forex know how hard it can be sometimes to walk away from the market. Still, it's necessary in order to become a successful trader.

Walking away can be especially difficult following a trade. This is because our emotions are running high and often get the best of us. But that's exactly what makes walking away at this time so beneficial.

After a profitable trade
After a win, we're feeling good about ourselves and our trading strategy. It feels like things are finally starting to click.

Walking away at this time can be tough. The natural tendency after a winning trade is to continue trading.

However, that's precisely why you should walk away.

Taking a break after a win will allow your emotions to settle. After the win, you're feeling excited and proud of yourself, and you have every right to be.

But as you may well know, pride and excitement can get you in a heap of trouble, and fast.

So the next time you have a winning trade, pat yourself on the back and then walk away. By the time you come back to your trading desk, your emotions will be under control and you'll be ready to approach the market with a neutral mindset.

After a losing trade
What do you do immediately following a loss?

I can't speak for you, but I know what I used to do. I would immediately start going through all my charts looking for a new setup with the intent of recovering what I just lost.

Whatever you do, don't do this. It's just your ego drawing you into one of the most common and costly traps in the Forex market.

If you're doing this, it means your emotions are getting the best of you.

Instead of seeing a loss as a reason to hop back in the market, take it as a signal to look at what you could have done differently. Remember, it's just feedback.

One reason the failure rate is so high in the Forex market is that traders haven't learned to lose.

Your emotions will always try to outweigh your logic after a loss; it's human nature. The key to becoming successful isn't about eliminating emotions after a loss, it's about channeling them in a way that will make you a better trader.

Top Forex traders know this and have learned how to control these emotions.

The very first step in controlling your emotions involves walking away for a bit.

This is when I do the bulk of my analysis anyway since I trade the daily time frame, so it makes sense to take a breather until then.

It's a simple, yet incredibly helpful, way of controlling your emotions.

8. They Don't Focus on Wins and Losses
Win vs lose
You can't visit a Forex site these days without seeing an advertisement for some strategy that promises a 98% win rate.

Why is that? Is it because a high win rate is needed to become a successful Forex trader?

Not even close!

They do it because it sells. People love to win, there's no denying it. If you've ever played sports or watched your favorite sports team on television, I'm sure you can relate.

Those behind the so-called strategy that produces an advertised 98% win rate know this and exploit it to make money.

Nobody is going to be enticed to spend money when they see a headline that promises a 50% win rate.

But what if it's a strategy with a proper risk to reward ratio that aims for $300 for every $100 risked?

At a 50% win rate, that's a 20% gain on a $5,000 account over the course of 10 trades.

Successful Forex traders know this. They have realized long ago that it's not about winning a high percentage of the time.

It's about maximizing the amount of money made on wins and minimizing the amount of money lost on losers.

As George Soros once said...

"It's not whether you're right or wrong, but how much money you make when you're right and how much you lose when you're wrong".

9. They Never Gave Up

Woman who never gave up

Although this one is last on the list, it's by far the most important to your success as a trader.

I've found over the years that many people, including Forex traders, lose sight of this very simple fact. The only way you can fail at becoming a successful Forex trader is if you give up.

This sounds obvious, but it amazes me how often I see perseverance and grit left off the list of reasons why a certain trader became successful.

You can't fail if you don't quit.

That brings us back to the first section of this post where I mentioned passion. You can't expect to achieve Forex success if you give up, and you can't expect to persevere if you don't have a passion for trading.

You must have a burning desire to want to succeed as a trader. Not because you want more money, but because you love trading.

Of all the ways to make money in this world, trading is arguably the worst choice.

That may surprise you coming from me, but of all the things I've accomplished in my life, none have come close to being as difficult and unforgiving as becoming a successful trader.

I don't say this to discourage you, but rather to prepare you for what's ahead.

In all honesty, although trading has been the most challenging endeavor I've ever undertaken, it's also been the most rewarding

Final Words

Whether you've been trading Forex for a month or five years, I hope the nine attributes of successful traders you just read will help you in your journey.

The most important takeaway from today's post is that there is no secret to successful Forex trading. Sure, there are various tips that can help you, but those who have achieved consistent profits are not untouchable.

In other words, there's nothing they do that you cannot eventually replicate.

However, if you intend to climb the ranks and join the top 5% of successful traders, you should be prepared to put in the work and devote the time necessary to succeed.

Embrace the journey, because there is no finish line. Even those who have achieved consistent profits have more to learn. Anything less wouldn't be worthwhile.

General FAQ

Can you get rich trading Forex?

I think the better question is: can you become consistently profitable trading Forex? The answer is a resounding, yes! The key is to focus on the process and forget about trying to strike it rich.

Focus on the process, stay disciplined, and the profits will follow.

Who is the most successful Forex trader? That depends on how you define "successful". For instance, is a billionaire who works 16 hour days and is generally unhappy more successful than someone who makes six figures a year but only works 6 hours a day and loves what they do? The second individual is more successful in my opinion.

CHAPTER ELEVEN

Managed Forex Trading

The managed forex trading is another type of trading in which the owner of the company works to stabilize you r amount and help you to have more profits. Tough the profits and the loss are not of their concern but still the forex managed system takes care of all these things. The forex managed system is involved in the case of profit and work to accomplish their targets and at the same time come out with better options for their clients. Thus the managed forex trading is beneficial to the customers as all their account are managed by the brokers and inform the about the profits which they have got in the whole transaction. Now let's read this article to find how the managed forex trading is done and the different forex managed systems.

The forex managed system consists of the clients who have their savings invested in some sort of deal or say in the currency trading. The work of the broker is to invest in the best company which is showing high rise and at the same time will tend to increase in terms of the profits. Thus when the transaction is complete you are bound to have profits. Thus with the help of the managed forex trading you can make as much profit as you want but everything must be done within the time limits and also with utmost care. As it is very difficult to invest in something new therefore the people who are new to this field can take help from a reliable broker who will help you out.

Therefore the managed forex trading is a good business if managed properly. The main aim of the managed trading is to efficiently manage the accounts of the clients and help them in all the possible way they can. The forex managed system proves to be best in every respect whether it is in working or in any other case. Then one must see that the trading is an important issue which requires skills and experience to handle each and every thing in proper way. With the help of the trading you ca not only carry out the currency exchange but also double and triple your invested amount.

CHAPTER TWELVE

Foreign Exchange Trading

The foreign exchange trading or more popularly the forex exchange consists of the exchange of the currencies of one country to the other. The forex foreign exchange is an international system through which the currencies are exchanged. The foreign exchange trading can be due to the several reasons. It may be either to increase the business or to establish a relationship between the two countries therefore the forex exchange tool is used which is very useful. The best thing about the forex foreign exchange is that as it is a standard body therefore there are no chances of frauds and other cases. Thus the transaction can be carried out in the safe way. Therefore if you do not know about the forex foreign exchange or the forex exchange then be sure to read this article which deals about it.

The forex exchange helps in determining the factors which can increase the cooperation of different countries. At the same time the forex foreign exchange is also beneficial in understanding the needs of the two countries thus facilitating the ease of work. With the help of the foreign exchange trading transfer of goods can take place easily and there will no problem in carrying out the business. Therefore the use of the foreign exchange trading will be helpful in every aspect whether it is in regards with the business as well as the personal relationships with the other countries. Thus it is important that the countries realize that it is necessary to build strong bonds with the other nations o cope up with the strategic problems.

The foreign exchange trading will not build bonds with the nations but also help in determining the necessary factors which will be useful in the long run. Apart from this the forex foreign exchange is done so that the imports and the exports of the commodity is done easily. Therefore you can understand the different issues which are related to the forex exchange. It has become the need of the hour and so it is important that one realized their importance only then the trading will prove to be fruitful in whichever way you want.

Forex Futures Trading

The forex futures includes the investments which are done for the future like some of them invest money currently but they want that it should begin after specified time. So the forex futures trading is one such deal which plans for the future. With the help of the futures trading you can invest amount for any specified period of time whenever you want. Therefore those who want that the investment must start after three months, they use the futures trading schemes which are very useful. Even the forex futures will help you to find the changes and study the entire time period. Thus the forex futures trading are mostly for those who want the investment to grow by leaps and bounds.

The forex futures trading are one such scheme which can provide you with the maximum profit as you get time to understand the market and the entire scenario. With the help of the forex futures one is able to get good understanding about the forex market and also the things that are going around. So it is obvious that the futures trading are the best. With lots of advantages all the people want to use the futures trading for the investment. Even the business can see a growth through the forex futures trading. The forex futures are therefore the ones who encourage the customers and tell them about the different schemes in which the investment is done.

The forex futures will definitely prove to the best as they are working very hard to make the future secure. Though there are chances of loosing but one must see the positive side of the forex futures trading. Therefore one can surely choose any of the futures trading schemes to avail the maximum benefit from the scheme. There are always better chances for improvement; unless you invest you will never get an idea as how the trading is carried out. Thus it becomes important to start such scheme which will definitely be beneficial in times to come. Hope the given information is appealing to you and at the same time valuable to you in all respect.

Forex Technical Analysis

The Foreign Exchange market is also known as forex. The forex market actually deals into multiple currencies and it is one of the largest markets across the world in the financial sector. Forex Training is just like the other types of investment trainings that are considered to be important so as to make your wining chances stronger. Undoubtedly the chances of securing huge profits here are fairly enough but one still needs to be more cautious while investing in to this volatile market. It is being advised that before applying to investment proposals one should make a forex analysis that can reveal the actual position of forex trading at a particular time. There are a number of analysis that are essential in order to excel in to this field and the forex technical analysis is jus one of them.

The forex technical analysis is actually the method of estimating the different price fluctuations and the likely to have trends in the future markets. This type of forex analysis is made in accordance with the past trends or the previous price movements. Here the charts are used to read the past facts and figures and the past actions are interpreted in accordance with the recent scenario. Typically the forex technical analysis means studying and analyzing the previous trends that have taken place a few days, weeks, months, years before. This type of forex analysis is conducted on the basis of the specific price of the currency that you are dealing in along with the volume that you have.

The forex technical analysis reveals that the prices have a definite trend in which they fall or rise. There are some few essential principles that are needed to draw the forex analysis conclusions. It has been said earlier that the forex technical analysis is based on the charts showing the previous statistics and other needed aspects. These charts have been designed by the skilled analysts who have complete knowledge and experience about the definite instruments and various market trends. So in a way this chart helps in making the forex analysis required for smooth sailing in the foreign exchange market.

CHAPTER THIRTEEN

Forex Trading Signals and pips

The forex signals are nothing but a sort of indication given to the companies through which they know that something unusual is going to happen. The forex trade signals are more like the alerts which are sending for some information or also for some changes that have occurred. Thus the use of the forex trading signals is done in both the positive and the negative sense. But it all depends upon the types of the alerts. The free forex signals are the ones which are developed free of cost and have no charges of you apply for them while there are some forex trading signals for which you have to pay some amount. Therefore it is the user's choice to subscribe for which forex signals. There are different types of free forex signals and the paid forex trade signals.

As you know that are several kinds of forex trade signals the users can choose the right one which can include the forex signals for the volume or he flash of light. Thus you will come across a variety of the forex trading signals. Even in the free forex signals you will find the different forex trade signals. Therefore with the use of the forex signals you can send messages to other centers and also get messages from the centers. Apart from the messages the information can also be exchanged by means of the forex trading signals. Thus you will different uses of the different free forex signals. Therefore it is seen that the alerts are very useful in case you need to indicate something to the other organization or the person.

The free forex signals are characterized by a feature which means that no cost has to be given so they are known as the free signals. Therefore with the forex trade signals you surely find some use as they are very much in demand and almost all companies use these forex signals for the benefit of the organization. Thus you don't require any extra for this set up but you can use the forex trading signals whenever you need them. But all you have to do is to subscribe for them and then they can be used for any type of work that you are interested in.

Forex Pips

The forex pip can be define as the small increment which is seen in any of the investment. The full form of the forex pip is percentage in point which means small changes in the prices or the rates. As these rates are small therefore they are known as the forex pips. The forex pips usually deal with the investment or with the currencies as well. Therefore this small change is very important as only a small change will be able to make a big difference. Then one must realize that even the small difference can be a major factor for the investment or the currency. Even in the currency you can find these changes. The forex pips are known as percentage in point as the rise is calculated in percentage therefore they are called as the forex pip.

The forex pip can be better understood like the change or the increment which is made when the prices of the currency rise. The forex pip is basically an increase therefore you will always have profits in case of the forex pips. So there is always a positive side of the forex pips. Therefore whenever you come to know about this forex rate then you must understand that the pip will definitely bring a change which is very necessary for those which have recently invested in such investments. Thus the entire result is based on the forex rate as the increment in the amount is also based on the type of investment that you have done.

Thus one cannot deny the fact that the forex pips are very useful in the long run as they can help you to provide the highest benefit that you can even think of. With the use of the forex pip there are always chances of prospects as you will come different types of schemes which will create difference particularly in the currencies. Even a small rise in the rate of the currencies can earn you the profits which are the final aim of making the investment. Therefore the above given information will surely benefit you in some way or the other.

CHAPTER FOURTEEN

Forex Trading Secrets and scalping

In order to be a successful trader or a broker there are few forex trading secrets which must be known to you. Whether you wish to become a trader or a broker but there are some tips whch are very useful for all the people who are a part of the forex market. The forex secrets include the attractive schemes and the strategies through which you get clients. The forex secrets also help the customers to establish good relationship with the customers so that they are able to understand the customer. With the help of the forex trading secrets you can carry out the task with the greatest ease and therefore you will be able to get the maximum customers who will want to join you.

The forex trading secrets also includes the tactics that are used by the brokers and the traders which prove helpful for the growth of the company. The forex secrets help the owners to know what the strategy of the competitors is and what kind of service they are providing. Therefore with the help of the forex secrets you can improve the quality of the service and hence the customers will be satisfied with you. So it is really important that attention is paid to all grounds whether it is the schemes or the quality of the service given to the clients. Even the forex trading secrets will be beneficial as they are used as the parameters for analyzing the performance of the organization.

Therefore the forex trading secrets are the best way to create an appealing inference for the people so that they are bound to choose your company. Through the forex secrets you will definitely get some profits as you will get the idea as to what has to be improved and what not. Certain measures can be taken to improve the services so that the clients are happy and always satisfied. Therefore it becomes important that one realize the need of the competition and how you can reach to the top most position with satisfied customers. Thus the need to evaluate yourself is fund and it must be done to improve oneself.
Forex Scalping

Forex trading is a type of investment which is similar to share market trading, the only difference being in volatility in nature. Here two international currencies are selected and they are purchased and sold depending on how they fare on ht international market as compared to the green back, which is dollar. One big advantage with the money market is that it is open 24X7, as the world is divided into different time zones and you can trade in currencies from the comfort of your own home at odd hours of the day. One of the popular methods of money trading is forex scalping in which the trader needs to make many small investments in a single day. Just like in a game of Cricket, where many batsmen score boundaries to increase their score, while others play safe and take single and twos to build their score. Scalping forex can be compared to somewhat this strategy.

Forex scalping gives good returns on your investments and that too quickly. Compared to conservative money trading, scalping forex has a higher risk-reward ratio. Any investor using forex scalping needs to set stop loss limits so that he does not suffer big losses in a single day. Another advantage is that there are no carry forward or outstanding trades at the end of the day. The disadvantages associated with scalping forex are higher commissions to the broker and the difficulty of the process as opposed to traditional trading. Alertness is that is the most important asset that is required from someone who does forex scalping. Sometimes scalper may need to take decision every 3-5 minutes. The rates of currencies keep on changing and the scalper needs to find entry and exit points for himself. Scalping forex requires short term trading and as such long term patterns are not required.

Scalpers can invest many times a day and hence can take home profits many times. Forex scalping requires one to be brave at heart and it is certainly not for someone faint at heart. Even brokers do not suggest you to go for scalping forex as it costs more and makes the business less attractive.

CHAPTER FIFTEEN

Forex Trading Charts And Quotes

Forex trading has emerged as a lucrative option to get attractive returns on you investments over the last few years. However the market is very volatile, and one needs to be alert all the time as the current exchange price of the currencies keeps on changing every few hours in respect to the standard currency that is the American dollar. There are a lot of things that a trader must look at, before investing his hard earned money at the money market.

forex trading charts and forex quotes are detailed descriptions of pairs of currencies . The movement of a particular currency in respect to another is clearly outlined in forex trading charts. Detailed study of forex trading charts is essential to be able to understand the intricacies of a currency movement in respect of another currency. forex trading charts provide you with intra day, daily weekly and monthly details of a particular currency. Any good website always gives forex quotes on a regular basis. Forex quotes need to be updated frequently as the entire business is dependent on the latest exchange price of forex trading charts a currency. Any delay in announcing forex quotes can cause losses for the investor as he may not be able to do the operations as desired. Absolutely minimum time is taken by the websites to provide forex quotes to the customers.

Those who are apprehensive of the Forex market as they fear of losing huge amount in the money market can now relax as there is the facility called mini forex trading. With mini forex trading people can start trading at the money market with very little amount. It is like getting the feel of the market without having to invest large sums of money. You can open a mini forex trading with as little as $300 and in addition you get the leverage from the broker. However, one needs to pay attention to mini forex trading as possible to his account even if it is mini forex trading as it is the building block of the larger investments in the market as you gain confidence in your transactions.

CHAPTER SIXTEEN

Forex Predictions and trading method More and more people the world over are turning to money market to make money as it has brought attractive returns on investments to millions of people. However, Forex market is very volatile and one has to be very careful lest he loses his entire money. There are some useful forex indicators which, if used wisely can bring you the desired results. There are some forex predictions which are based on careful analysis of the previous trends of the currency with respect to the greenback and they can be very fruitful when engaging in operations in the money market. Forex history pertains to all the data connected to the currency you are interested in trading and its previous showings.

Using the forex indicators, forex predictions and forex history does not guarantee of huge profits instantly. It only means that doing your homework prior to carrying out the operations in the Forex market will certainly minimize the risk factor to a great extent. Having a deep and sound knowledge of the forex predictions and forex indicators is critical to carrying out the operations in the money market. Most Forex software that are available in the market come along with forex indicators. These forex indicators can be extremely helpful while trading at the market. Forex predictions software is available in the market which can predict in advance which way the market will move and thus it will help you to make more money. Forex predictions software is the best thing to happen to forex trading as it makes sure you don't pull the trigger when you are completely wrong.

Forex history is an important part of your preparations while dealing in the money market. It tells in detail with the help of graphs and charts, the actual movement of the currency you wish to deal in. One needs to study the forex history deeply before investing in the money market. Forex market is very volatile and any lapse on your part can result in heavy losses for you. So it is essential to carefully analyze the forex history before investing in the money market.

Forex Trading Method

Forex trading has become very popular today with more and more people jumping on to the Forex market to make money. However, Forex markets are very volatile, and one needs to be alert all the time to be able to reap the rewards in the money market. To derive maximum forex profit from your forex funds you need to follow certain guidelines using forex arbitrage and forex hedging. The method in Forex trading where an investor tries to take advantage of the inefficiency in the pairing currencies is known as forex arbitrage. In forex arbitrage, you buy a currency from a market and try to sell it in another market trying to take advantage of the anomaly of its price in the two markets which occurs for a very short period of time. Forex arbitrage should be used only as an exception and not as a rule. How to make use of forex arbitrage is something that requires deep knowledge of the working of different markets and you should use it with caution.

Forex hedging is another strategy or tool for deriving better profits from the money market. Forex hedging is not easy to put in practice and should be adopted only if you are a regular or seasoned player in the money market. Forex hedging requires a large amount of capital. Forex hedging is certainly not for a novice or for someone who cannot afford to lose heavily in the money market.

Forex markets are just like share markets, the only difference being the timings of the two. Unlike share markets, you can use your forex funds 24X7 as the world is divided into different time zones and you can carry your operations at odd hours from the comfort of your home. The more forex funds you use, more is the forex profit. It is really easy to make forex profit with forex funds if you remain alert. forex profit from your forex funds depends upon your correct knowledge of the current exchange price of the currency. With a little experience, you can make huge forex profit from the money market.

CHAPTER SEVENTEEN

Forex Megadroid Robots And Metatrader

If you have money to invest then there is the forex market waiting for you where you can get attractive returns on your money. Here you can buy and sell different currencies based on their current exchange price in terms of the standard currency which is the American dollar. Forex metatrader or Forex megadroid is a platform that is provided by the brokers to you to trade in currencies. There are numerous platforms but forex metatrader has been found to be the most effective when it comes to earning in the money market. There are many who have the money but not the time to deal in the money market. Then there are people who are novices and don't know much about Forex. For these people, new software has been designed which is called forex robots or forex trading robots. Forex robots and forex trading robots are tools which look after the operations in the money market on your behalf and you need not worry about your investments. There are many types of forex trading robots or forex robots but the most popular ones are the forex megadroid and forex metatrader.

Forex megadroid and forex metatrader work much in the same way as the human brain. You just need to feed the correct values of exit and stop loss and they perform all the tasks needed to operate in the money market. These forex robots or forex trading robots have been designed to work in real time conditions and they have been tested in all the situations. Forex megadroid and forex metatrader as automated forex robots have earned their owners a lot of money.

In my opinion, no machine can compare with human brain, and to ask forex robots or forex trading robots to look after your investments, that too in a volatile market like Forex is not feasible. Though one can take the help of forex megadroid occasionally as when there is an emergency, asking forex trading robots to keep on generating profits for you day after day is not the correct approach. It is always better to face the market yourself.

www.ingramcontent.com/pod-product-compliance
Lightning Source LLC
Chambersburg PA
CBHW051423150726
48000CB00005B/1931